THE DOUGHNUT DIARIES

THE DOUGHNUT DIARIES

A Personal Trainer's Tale of Being Every Size From 12 Through 0

Rachel Lavin

YouSpeakIt
PUBLISHING
*The Easy Way
to Get Your Book
Done Right*™

ISBN: 978-1-945446-94-8

My book is dedicated to every single one of you who, like me, has spent your entire life hating your body. I hope my story inspires and supports you so you finally see you are not alone—you never were.

Praise for
The Doughnut Diaries

"This book takes you down the road less traveled—the one where you are kind to your body and give it what it needs to stay in good mental and physical health, and Rachel is the perfect guide. With her honest and unfiltered stories, you will feel like you have a teammate on your own personal journey to true happiness and acceptance of your body."

— Kari Simpson

Global Retail Marketing Director

"Every single woman knows how it feels to put your body through the ringer to achieve an unhealthy goal of perfection that is not sustainable. Now, Rachel Lavin reveals her journey in figuring out how to maintain a healthy body and enjoy life with *The Doughnut Diaries!*"

— Anahita Crawford

Head of Diversity, Equity & Inclusion (DEI) Executive,

Sr. DEI consultant and Coach,

former global DEI executive at Nike

"If you have been ignoring your body and its needs for far too long then let *The Doughnut Diaries* bring you back to your Self."

— Rawa Alhoty
Talent Experience Leader at Coinbase
former Talent Acquisition Manager at Nike

"I like to call Rachel's book a necessity for anyone who is struggling with being image conscious. I highly suggest that you read this uplifting, informative book that also expresses Rachel's great sense of humor. Each passage in the book is not only very true, but will hit the spot for readers as they relate to Rachel's journey on how she successfully overcame the dark side of what we're led to believe we should look like."

— Tonijean Kulpinski, CBHC, BCHP, AADP
Bestselling Author of the
Stop Battling Disease & Start Building Wellness Book Series

"Rachel Lavin is east coast through and through—right from the intro in *The Doughnut Diaries* her witty humor jumps off the page, and her colorful language is refreshing!"

— Christina Thornton
Executive Producer/formerly at
Victoria's Secret and Guess, Inc.

Contents

CHAPTER FIVE

Acknowledgments

I would like to thank:

The love of my life. You are the true meaning of what a life partner is; you are my best friend. Thank you for all the firsts in our relationship; they are endless. Thank you for showing me that you love me every day.

My family. I'm so grateful for the bond that I share with you all in different ways. I've always felt loved, supported, guided, and enlightened by you. You make me who I am, and I love you all.

My beautiful, funny, loyal girlfriends. Together we have shared more than twenty years of honest and insightful conversations, laughing so hard we peed, and cried too many tears to count. These have been some of the best times of my life. I love you all, and I truly know how lucky I am to know such amazing women.

My clients, past, present, and future. You've taught me how to listen without judgment, how to be an example of empathy and truth, and how to be a supportive and fearless personal trainer. Because of you, I will always do my best.

To my peers and mentors. There have been so many of you over my twenty-year career, and I know I've learned something from you all. I have been supported, encouraged, and influenced by you in many ways. I've learned that the fitness industry has more than enough room for all of us to shine. I hope we continue to teach each other, learn from each other, and support each other. It's important that we show the next generation of fitness professionals how it's done.

To Babypie Publishing: You *all* made this experience so wonderful and easy. I *loved* the process, and thanks to you, I now have a best-selling book!

Myself. After so many years of hating my body, I am finally able to send my story into the world from a place of healing and love. I had to surrender myself to the process and do the hard work to become a strong, positive woman who truly wants the best for herself. I'm so grateful that I'm now able to see my body and myself through the eyes of love 97.7 percent of the time; my promise to myself is to continue striving for 100 percent.

Finally, to my readers: Thank you for reading my story. I only hope to inspire you to love your body and to know that you are not alone.

Introduction

This book describes almost four decades of not having the self-confidence, self-acceptance, and self-esteem to love my body or to love myself. In these pages, I share my experiences of dealing with all my weight gains and losses from a young age through my late forties.

Having attempted to write this book many times, I am now coming from a place of continued healing and love instead of a place of shame and guilt. Every time I lost the weight, I would think about doing this book: *Look at me! I'm finally keeping the weight off.* Then, the weight would come back every single time and so would the disappointment.

I have been every size: 12, 10, 8, 6, 4, 2, and a *zero*. My weight has fluctuated so many times throughout my life. I had no idea who I was or who I wanted to be; I was only my body. My mind was constantly consumed with how I looked or how I didn't fit in anywhere because my body was never right for any situation. I constantly put myself down in front of others, shrinking and isolating myself. Since I turned forty, I've worked to know myself and heal from more than forty years of hating my body. I finally feel like I can share the real me with you.

My name is Rachel. By the time this book hits the shelves, I will be fifty years old. I've chosen the last year of my forties to finally share my story. I sometimes look in the mirror and cannot believe I have been on this Earth for forty-nine years. Where has the time gone?

I think about the many years I wasted not being able to love and accept my body. I cut myself some slack because I simply did not know how to love my body then. The wonderful part of my story is that now I *do* know how, and I get to spend the next fifty years absolutely loving my body and myself.

I have been on diets, restricting foods and exercising, for most of my life. I have lost and gained weight more times than I can count. This will not be the only time I'll tell you I have been a size twelve and a size zero and every size in between. I have also experienced every emotion that comes from weight loss and weight gain. I was consumed by thoughts of my body. For many years, I believed there was nothing more than how I or others saw my body, but since turning forty, I've been on a path to self-discovery and self-love. It's been quite the decade.

This path wasn't easy; it took hard fucking work. I needed to realize that I was my own worst enemy and if I wanted to be truly happy—to have peace and enjoy the rest of my life—it would have to start with me. I needed to change my mindset, my attitude, and how I talked to and about myself as I referenced my body.

As you read, remember that the numbers on a scale or a clothing tag aren't the most important parts of my story.

How I saw myself and my body image affected most of my life. I continue to do the work every day. I am not perfect. I never will be perfect, but I am happy.

I invite you to read my book without self-judgment. Read my story and keep beaming with delight and jumping for joy because you know you are not alone. After years of hating my body, I now believe in myself and trust my body, and so can you.

I have read quite a few inspirational books, and they have been amazing tools on my journey. However, I wanted you to relate to my story in a way that might have eluded you before. So, don't worry about stopping to write in a journal for thirty minutes, or making charts or lighting candles. Be in the moment and feel your feelings. I've learned that we all absorb information differently, and what works for one person doesn't work for another.

Please enjoy my story; read it with an open heart and an open mind. We are all in this together, and I'm here to share my experience openly and honestly with you. I want to inspire you and show you it is possible to stop the madness of dieting, restricting foods, or using exercise to make yourself smaller. It is attainable for you to love your body right now at any size.

My hope is for you to learn to love your shape and feel powerful in the body that you are in today. If a woman who has been through the ups and downs of losing and gaining weight her whole life can find inner peace and finally love her body at any size, then so can you. It's never too late to believe in yourself.

Once you finish reading this book, I hope there is no doubt in your mind, and you will be able to say with conviction: *I am not alone, and I'm in a body that I love right now.*

Chapter One

Dieting, Restricting, and Bingeing, *Oh My!*

There is nothing more important to true growth than realizing that you are not the voice of the mind—you are the one who hears it.

~ Michael A. Singer

SEARCHING FOR SOMETHING

This quote reflects my experience with dieting, restricting, and bingeing through every decade of my life. Over and over, I have done whatever it took to have a small body.

Perhaps, you have thought:

- *Only I feel this way.*
- *Only I know how hard it is not to eat these bad foods.*
- *Only I can't keep this fucking weight off.*

Read on and realize you aren't the only one who struggles with obsessing over food and how it affects the size of your body. We all feel as if no one else understands how hard this is. Just keep this statement in the front of your mind:

You are not alone.

For me, it started at birth. During the first few years of my life, my parents were told I had cystic fibrosis, an incorrect diagnosis. I was put on medication, and the main side effect was weight gain. I still have baby pictures in which I was nothing but a little cinnamon roll. I was a toddler by the time the doctors realized I did not have the disease and could be taken off the medication.

Some of that weight did fall off, but this experience charted the course for a lifelong relationship with my body. I didn't realize it yet, but those first few years of my life taught me how to fight with my body. I can't remember exactly what my everyday diet was like except for the one rule my mother had: no sugary cereals were allowed in our house.

When I realized I wasn't allowed to have certain foods at such a young age, I knew that restricting foods has always been a part of my life. Anytime I had the opportunity to eat the *one thing* I wasn't allowed to eat at home, I binged and binged hard. At this young age, I'm sure it wasn't about the weight. Yet, I now see how restricting and bingeing carried into my adulthood, and until recently, the two went hand in hand.

Any diet by any name instills restriction in us, and in all honesty, there are too many out there to list, so I will not list them here. All my dieting really did was reinforce restriction, and I built my entire existence and belief system on restricting food, then bingeing.

The 80s and 90s were my two decades of fad diets, from the SlimFast shakes to diet pills to never eating bread. The following two decades of the 2000s consisted of celebrity diets in magazines, juice cleanse diets, and still not eating any bread. All those crazy diets are still around; they just have better branding. Now they are called *lifestyles*, and we know them as *paleo*, *keto*, and *intermittent fasting*.

I believed all these outlandish dieting rules and applied them to my own life over and over. I was imprisoned by these restrictive food rules until 2019.

Blissfully Restricting

I was still living life believing that it was perfectly normal to restrict most foods, and I even passed those beliefs on to my clients.

Remember the expression: *suddenly, a light bulb went off?*

Well, I heard myself tell a female client something I've told my clients on a regular basis: *Don't eat a banana after our workout because it has too much sugar.*

As the words left my lips, my immediate afterthought was: *What the fuck am I saying?*

In a single rush of truth, it hit me, and I knew right then and there that I still believed false dieting rules. Unfortunately, I expected my clients to do the same. Someone told me not to eat carrots because they have too much sugar, and I guess the list just grew from there. Foods that come from Mother Earth were deemed bad because of their sugar content. Seriously?!

So *what* if fruits and vegetables have natural sugar! This extreme shit keeps circling around in diet culture, and we continue to live by it. Please open your eyes and think for yourself: *Does this make any fucking sense?*

Diets change their packaging all the time and promise us some magic potion that will make this diet finally work. Every single diet in the world has only one goal: to teach us that our bodies aren't good enough the way they are and that we will never be happy without being on a diet to achieve thinness. It's been drilled into our brains from the youngest age that we must always be on a diet; it's literally our society's normal state for everyone to be restricting some kind of food in order to be the smallest we can possibly be, taking up the least amount of space possible.

All for what? Have any of us truly been happy living this way?

What's in Your Fridge?

For most of my life, my diet consisted of processed and packaged garbage. My refrigerator and pantry were only stocked with products that were fat-free, sugar-free, taste-free, salt-free, or had the word diet on the label. If there were vegetables in my fridge, they were those salads in a bag, and my freezer was always stocked with prepared meals of some kind.

Looking back on the way I learned to eat, I can understand why my body was a hotbed of inflammation and weight gain. Even though these were the types of foods in my life, I still believed things like pasta, bread, and sweets were the only foods I couldn't eat because they were the fat makers. All my attention and energy were always focused on restricting some type of food or entire food groups.

This is how I grew up, and I know I'm not alone. A lot of us grew up with a similar diet. The cycle has repeated itself for decades. I believed with every ounce of my being this cycle was completely normal. Once it dawned on me that I was still living every day on this messy and unfulfilling diet merry-go-round, I wanted off. Immediately!

I didn't want to waste any more time being unsatisfied with the small list of foods I actually allowed myself to eat; I wanted to enjoy everything. That shift meant I had to think for myself and reprogram more than four decades of dieting and restricting. Food had been my enemy, as I had lived in a constant state of fear that I was only going to gain weight if I wasn't constantly restricting my food intake. I was undernourishing my body instead of letting it do what it is designed to do: *eat*.

Waking Up Is the Fun Part

In the last half of 2019 and well into 2020, I made a conscious decision to stop restricting everything and anything. Nothing was off limits. I had to relearn every single thing I'd been told about food my entire life and start over. I wanted better for myself and for my clients. No more shame, no more punishment, and no beating myself up because I ate a fucking doughnut!

I had to come to terms with my smaller body changing. Was I going to be okay? Could I be happy if my body changed?

But then I asked myself: *Was I actually happy before, even when I was in a smaller body?* The answer was no.

I had been consumed by dieting, restricting, and bingeing for forty-nine years, and I was exhausted. I wanted to eat foods that nourished my entire body. I wanted to eat foods because I enjoyed their taste. It's okay to associate foods with feelings; they can bring back fond memories, such as that warm and cozy feeling associated with a piping-hot bowl of homemade chili. Sometimes, it's simply because that doughnut looks too good not to eat.

I spent way too many years not eating an extremely long list of foods I thought were going to make my body bigger.

For what?

So I could fit inside the bubble of what I was taught my body was supposed to look like. I'm hopeful that the truth speaks louder than any diet's claims or promises. Diets only provide temporary results. The weight never stays off, and diets will never work the same way twice.

We are constantly trying the latest and greatest new diet to achieve what we already have—the right body. Here's a more valuable truth: every single diet is impossible to sustain long term, and they all suck.

THE DIET THAT CHANGED MY LIFE

I know you're saying to yourself: *Why is she telling me about some big life-changing diet after she just told me to give double middle fingers to dieting?*

This is so much more than a diet; it's the part of my story that turned my life 180 degrees from who I was to who I am. It helped me realize I knew nothing about taking care of myself physically or mentally. It sparked the desire to learn about myself and why I kept repeating the same patterns.

This experience helped me to grow into a self-sufficient adult, which encouraged me to learn more about where I came from and why I was running from everything and everyone. It provided me the whole-body-and-mind healing that lit my path to self-discovery and prompted me to ask myself: *Who am I?*

I feel like we all have that moment in life when we are presented with a choice to stay the same person we've always been or to grow into the person we were meant to be. This time was a pivotal lesson, and it completely changed me. I learned how to listen to my body's signals and how to nourish my body with real food. No juice cleanses or packaged diet food this time.

Until this experience, I had no idea how to cook a lick of food. I could microwave a low-cal frozen dinner, but I had no interest in cooking. I couldn't follow a recipe, and I hated touching raw food.

In 2008, I was a single woman living in a 400-square-foot studio apartment. I was trying to experience everything New York City had to offer, including a social life. After all, my dream was to live in the Big Apple, but I was still extremely uncomfortable in my own skin and always so unhappy with how my body looked.

I began working at a boutique gym in Manhattan. I loved my job there; it was such a great place with great people. Even though Club H is long gone, I'm fortunate to know some wonderful people because of that place. Honestly, in my entire twenty-plus-year career, it remains my second-favorite job as a personal trainer.

In 2011, Club H was sold and came under new management, and the new owners thought that pushing our personal training program would be the key to the gym's success. They launched a 90-day fitness challenge. At the time, 30-day and 90-day challenges were gaining popularity on social media. We were told to pick a member and train them for ninety days for free. The catch was they had to post a picture of every single thing they ate on Facebook—no exceptions. The individual had frequent weigh-ins and was required to post those results as well. Sounds fun, huh?

I'll never forget the day my then fitness manager sat me down in the office and asked me if I was happy. Oh boy, I knew where this conversation was going; it wasn't the first time I was spoken to about my body. He proceeded to tell me that I needed to look the part of a personal trainer. He told me that I should do the 90-day fitness challenge along with the other members.

He said, in his usual overexcited way, "Jump on the scale right now. Let's see where you're at!"

My insides contracted in fear, and my palms began to sweat. *NO. I don't want to!*—the little girl inside my head screamed. But I stepped on. *Why is that number flashing 170!? It's not going to land there. There is no fucking way!* But it did. I knew I had put on weight again, but 170 pounds!?

I'm a five-foot-three woman, and I was taught—like everyone else on the planet—that number equaled obesity. I remember the way I felt seeing the highest number of my life on that scale. It was scary and painful, and I was totally ashamed by that 170-pound number staring back at me. I was devastated by how fat I was, and I immediately burst into tears.

Truthfully, my diet was shit. I still ate like a teenager—eating out, grabbing the first thing I saw, skipping meals completely, and living on protein shakes. My body was seriously rebelling, so I was bloated and uncomfortable most of the time. I know now that I was experiencing a severe case of inflammation along with the weight gain. I needed to help myself, but I didn't know how. I had no clue how to handle situations or people like that one.

I would leave most similar encounters feeling like my heart was breaking, and I was always in tears.

I would walk away thinking:

- *Why does this person not like me?*
- *What did I do?*
- *Why are they finding fault in me, in my body?*

After the hurt came anger because I would feel so betrayed. As a result, that person would be cut out of my life forever. I repeated this painful but very real cycle for years.

During this time, I was incapable of loving my body or myself. I was always looking outside myself for approval, and I could never trust anyone in my life because I didn't trust myself. Since then, I've learned that I was so easily hurt by other people because I did not know my value as a person. I've worked hard to deal with the pain and trauma surrounding me as a person and about my body.

I'm able to see the world more clearly, and I know I can respond differently today. I recognize how sheltered I really was; I didn't have the life skills of an independent woman. I had no idea where to begin, but that was all going to change.

I was introduced to a wonderful nutritionist, Lyn-Genet Recitas, without her and her nutrition program—The Plan, my journey would not have ended up the way it did. I hired Lyn to help me lose weight, but she did more than that. Lyn guided me into becoming a self-sufficient woman. This wasn't a diet like I'd ever experienced before. I needed to learn how to buy and cook my own food and to learn how to pay attention to my body's signals.

I needed to learn how to differentiate my body's responses to the things I ate, discovering the difference between feeling satisfied and full and when something I ate disrupted homeostasis, causing an inflammatory response, such as pain or discomfort. She taught me how to put ingredients together and make meals that tasted great and left me with so much energy.

I found myself sleeping better. I felt less bloated, and even my period changed. The weight began falling off. My entire existence didn't change with the snap of my fingers, though. I put in the hard work, and day one was no joke.

Where's a Machete When You Need One?

The conversation going on in my head that first morning of my life-changing diet was full of constant loud chatter.

You must do this.

You can't be fat anymore.

Will I get fired if I don't lose the weight?

Whole Foods better have all this healthy shit on my shopping list.

She told me I could lose fifty pounds. Is that possible?

I've never lost fifty pounds all at once.

All these thoughts were running around in my head in the time it took me to reach the bottom of the escalator. Once I stepped off and was inside Whole Foods, I pulled out the 300-page shopping list from my pocket. I looked up and my eyes began blinking frantically; I was being blinded by a sea of bright oranges, greens, reds, and yellows. When I finally focused, I realized I was standing in a massive produce section.

Holy shit!

Did you know there are eighty different types of apples and sixteen types of lettuces? I'd only been there for thirty seconds, and my eyes were already welling with tears. I took a good look around this mammoth store, as it was more than my brain could handle.

I couldn't move, my feet were cemented onto the floor, and I could hear myself screaming inside my head: *FUCK! What in the hell has this woman done to me?*

I looked down at my list, and I did a double take. *Wait—is this in English?* I blinked away the tears and refocused on my list. It was English, but 95 percent of the list consisted of items I'd never heard of before. My brain tried to process it, and the inner chatter grew even *louder.*

Where in the hell am I supposed to put all this food?

How am I going to follow a recipe with ingredients I've never even heard of before?

I don't have room in my tiny-ass, Barbie-doll-sized fridge for all this food.

I reminded myself why I was doing this and forced myself to breathe. I thought: *I need to breathe or else I'm going to get back on that escalator, ride up to the street, and stay fat! I can't do that. No, this time I must keep off the weight.*

I wanted this new plan to work so much that I was willing to learn how to grocery shop and cook. I looked back down at the list and saw Swiss chard. *What in the actual fuck is Swiss chard?* I saw more words that were supposed to be foods, but I couldn't be sure:

- Shallots
- Zucchini
- Baby romaine
- Orange zest
- Whole ginger
- Butternut squash
- Turmeric
- EVOO (extra virgin olive oil)

In that moment, I prayed to God that a giant machete would magically appear in my hands so I could march through every aisle and chop every single item in Whole Foods a new asshole. Tears were streaming down my face in utter frustration and fear, which was my normal way of dealing with the unknown. I gathered what I could find—or at least what I thought was good enough—and got the hell outta there. I swear to you that first trip to Whole Foods took over two hours.

Now, I'm Supposed to Cook

Once I finally got all my food back to my apartment, then came the cruel and unusual punishment of trying to figure out which ingredients I needed to make my homemade fucking soup. I stared down at all the food for what seemed like eternity, and then realized I had to start because this shit wasn't going to cook itself. I was supposed to make an actual meal from a recipe. *Help!*

I'll be honest. The first thousand attempts at cooking food for myself were unbelievably hard, and most results tasted like shit. I burned a lot of stuff, undercooked chicken, and overcooked sweet potatoes. But I didn't give up. I kept cooking until it became a part of me.

Looking back, I can now laugh at what a lunatic I was in the kitchen. I made some pretty awful meals. These days, I feel so much more confident in the kitchen, and I truly enjoy cooking. I can actually follow a recipe and make some signature dishes. My food tastes great! So not only can I make delicious meals for my boyfriend and me, I even trust myself enough to cook for my friends and family and say with confidence that I won't send them to the emergency room with food poisoning.

Did You Say Size Zero?

I did end up losing about fifty pounds while on that diet. I was able to get my weight down from 170 to 125 pounds for a short amount of time. It took about nine months to lose all that weight. That was the first time in my life I was able to fit into a size zero. I won't lie to you. Fitting into a size zero pair of jeans was pretty fantastic.

Of course, there are still times that I miss being in a smaller body, now that I am no longer a size zero. That is a real emotion; one I still feel sometimes. I allowed myself to mourn my smaller body and be sad because my smaller clothes didn't fit anymore.

Just because I've decided to be happy and love my body at any size, please don't interpret that choice as meaning I don't care about my health. Wanting to be a whole person means I still take pride in my overall appearance. I still color my hair, wax my eyebrows, shave my legs, and wear makeup. The most important thing I do for myself and my body is exercise, which I will talk more about in the next chapter. I'll say it now, and then I'll say it again: loving my body at whatever size means I continue to nourish it with foods that make me happy and exercise that makes me feel my best.

FOOD WAS SCARY

After all these years, I realized that fear was my motivation for going on countless diets. I restricted the amount of food as well as the types of foods because I lived in constant fear of being fat. I believed that being fat was why I felt unloved, unhappy, and socially unacceptable. I told myself that if I could keep off the weight, I would be happy, and people would finally love and accept me.

I didn't know that it was me who didn't love myself. No one in my life ever made a bigger deal about the size of my body than I did. I always resented the weight. I hated being fat, and it was excruciatingly hard to lose the weight. I could never keep it off for very long. This cycle continued for most of my life. I didn't understand the necessity of nourishing my body with a variety of foods and the correlation with moving my body in the most efficient way. This lack of understanding was my downfall.

I had to recognize that my body needed food every day, and I needed to move my body every day. Food, movement, and rest are now the keys to my success. I finally get it—how important all three are—and I know now that my body needs all three of those things to be its best self. I've tried and tested one without the other so many times and failed miserably every time.

It's awful that we have passed hurtful, painful diet lies down to every generation. I know that men experience these lies as well, so I'm including them too.

It's my opinion that fitness professionals give out the worst nutritional and exercise advice, and, in turn, sometimes follow this advice more than our clients. I know this was true for me. I needed to start thinking for myself and let the truth sink in: We are not all meant to have the same body, to look the same, eat the same foods, or move our bodies the same way. We all need to eat and move in a way that makes us feel our best.

I endured so much anxiety over the years because of cookie-cutter diets. I believed that if I would only follow a certain diet and exercise program, I would have a tiny, sculpted body with a flat stomach, no cellulite, and, in turn, be extremely happy. My peers and society taught me the unrealistic expectation that I should achieve the perfect body, according to their standards. I never once considered what it was doing to my body on the inside or dared to ask if it was good for me. I didn't ask if my body was even capable of looking like someone else's body.

Countless times, I forced myself to say no to foods I loved because I felt I would be judged for eating something *fattening*. Then, the pressure would grow until I would binge on every food that would stand still because I couldn't stop thinking about that slice of cake I had denied myself a few days before.

I spent my whole life listening to anyone or anything other than myself on what foods I should eat or how I should move my body. I was constantly reminded what foods would make me fat or keep me fat and unhealthy. I never had to look far for a diet that promised it would shed pounds and inches off my waistline.

I find it fascinating that we love fatness as long as it's on a baby or a puppy. Rolls and rolls of fat are adorable on them, but pop culture tells us it's disgusting on an adult human body.

We can't live like this anymore. Don't be an asshole to yourself or anyone else. Eat that slice of cake!

All Diets Work Once

Of course, all diets work in the beginning. If they didn't, we wouldn't always be on one. I believed being on a diet was going fix me, and boy, did I need fixin' because I didn't have the body the world expected me to have. I always felt betrayed by my body. *Why couldn't it just stay fucking skinny?*

The real bitch is that *all* diets do work at first, and that's why I was always going back on one. When I forced myself to restrict, eat less, and stop eating certain foods completely, my body had no choice but to respond. Initially, I would lose some weight, but my body would realize what I was doing to it and hold on desperately to the small number of calories I provided and stop functioning properly. The color of my skin would look gray, or I would break out; my hair would look and feel dry. I'd go days without a poop, and my mood would be utter shit.

Of course. I would grow hungrier and crabbier until I couldn't stand it anymore, and off to my favorite Mexican restaurant I would go to shovel into my face a basket of chips and salsa plus a combo platter of chicken or beef tacos and enchiladas with rice and beans. The entire meal could feed a family of four, but it would be gone in a matter of a few minutes.

I can laugh about those times now because, thankfully, I don't do that to myself anymore. I listen to my body and my hunger signals. I understand now why there wasn't enough space in my brain for anything else back then. I was so emotionally drained that I couldn't focus on school, work, or my relationships because I was always so obsessed about my body size, my food intake, and everything I had to do to try to be smaller.

After years of this cycle, I chose to take a hard look at why I wasn't satisfied with my body and why I constantly felt the need to change it. I am still working on having a healthy relationship with all foods, and I still experience hard days when I want to go back to my old ways of restricting my food intake.

Sharing my story means telling you the truth, even if it isn't pretty. I still have days where I have negative thoughts or reactions to the sight of my body or the feeling of more weight on my body or having to buy clothes in a bigger size. It's real, and it's tough, especially after spending close to a year in quarantine due to COVID-19. I haven't seen the inside of a gym in almost a year, and I've gained weight and lost muscle.

However, I remind myself that even in the midst of a pandemic, my desire to stay happy and whole wins over those temporary feelings. I continue to eat when I am hungry and move my body in the little home gym my boyfriend and I have made for ourselves. We are doing the best we can with what we have.

The days when I do relapse into my old thoughts, I console myself, tell myself I'm okay, and remind myself to be grateful

I still have a body that can move. Some days all I can muster is to tell my body: *I love you.* Then on other days, it's even harder, and there are tears. I do my best to not allow negative self-talk, including these words I sometimes want to scream in my head: *You're so fat!*

I'm human, and I have lived in a thin world thinking I had a fat body for forty-plus years. These thoughts may never go away entirely, but I will continue to grow stronger and respond to myself with love and patience until they do. I also remind myself that it's okay to mourn my smaller, thinner body as long as I don't live in that mourning. Missing my smaller body is a part of this process, but I also know that small body wasn't my healthiest or happiest body either.

Having more weight on me is an adjustment, but it doesn't mean I'm bad or that I have failed. I choose to stay grateful during this crazy time and tell myself that I'm allowed to eat multiple times a day. I need to eat food every day for the rest of my life. I need to let go of my negative relationship with food and remember that even the most evolved diet is still a diet, and I'm in a body that's worthy of self-love right now.

Getting Skinny Versus Staying Skinny

Wanting to be accepted and loved by my friends, by men, by my family—hell, by strangers—was always my motivation for starting a new diet or going back to a previous diet.

It may have been earlier in my life, but I first recall becoming very self-conscious of my body in sixth grade. I had already started developing breasts and had started my period before the other girls. My thighs touched and my belly protruded. It was at this time that I really remember starting to obsess about my body. I also began noticing the bodies of other girls and how different mine was. Honestly, I don't remember the first day I started dieting or when that word became a part of me; it just did. My dieting merry-go-round grew to be the essence of who I was becoming, and trying to change my body became my number one goal in life.

Growing up, I didn't know any women or girls my age who had a positive body image. It's unfortunate to think back and see how hating my body stole so much from me. It left me vulnerable to people who thought it was their business to tell me what to do with my body. Over the years, everyone—from my family members, friends, boyfriends, to my coworkers and bosses—has made comments about my body; they told me that I needed to lose weight or work on this body part or that body part too many times to count.

During my career as a personal trainer, I've been shamed on social media by my peers for my food choices and told to my face that my body wasn't the right size to be a personal trainer. Of course it hurt, but I had to learn that it was because of the way I saw myself that I constantly accepted someone else's idea of who I was supposed to be. I'm so grateful for knowing now, at this stage in my life, that this is all complete bullshit!

In my experience, being a female personal trainer in a big city leaves your body vulnerable to much scrutiny. After the last big diet I shared with you earlier, many people had witnessed my transformation, and that came with a whole new set of opinions from people. There was a constant barrage of comments from coworkers and clients, and because I worked in a gym, members felt like it was perfectly okay to comment on my body.

There was a daily slew of comments like these:

You look amazing.

You're so small!

You look so beautiful.

Look at your new body!

You skinny bitch!

The last one was always the worst because it made me feel like they were angry with me for the way I looked. At the time, women around me actually told me how jealous they were of my weight loss. I never felt comfortable with all the attention; it never felt real. I know I had to experience all these different stages to be able to share my story, but it's also shown me how much we are obsessed with body size. Praise regarding weight loss can be addicting, but it can also be detrimental, and that's the truth.

Just because I can force my body to be 125 pounds by putting myself through extreme and drastic restriction of food doesn't mean I should. Living this way was all-consuming, and it sucked all the joy out of my life. I spent each and every waking moment thinking about my food intake and how much exercise I had to do in a day, and as if that wasn't enough, I would have dreams about how to keep myself small. By the time I declared a big *fuck this!* to dieting and restricting the foods I could or couldn't eat, I was exhausted from giving all of my energy to thinking about my body. It was an endless cycle, and I just didn't want to do it anymore.

I hope I'm being clear; just because I'm no longer fixated on being a skinny bitch and I don't restrict my food any longer *doesn't mean I've given up on myself.* My health is a priority for me. How my body feels and moves through the rest of my life is extremely important to me. I continue to strive to be the best version of myself, but I am choosing *me* and my happiness and well-being over any societal idea of my body! I hope you will too.

Dieting and Control

Once I decided to stop obsessing over the size of my body, I was able to see what a controlling person I was. Constantly dieting was just another way that I tried to control my surroundings, my emotions, and the way people treated me. I know that I wasn't kind to myself or to others. I see how focusing only on my outside appearance and wanting to have the perfect body consumed me.

I thought if I were in a smaller body, men would be more attracted to me, my friends would invite me to all the social events; I would finally be accepted. Instead, it made me into a real selfish person. I had an unrealistic outlook on life, and I made everything so much harder than it needed to be.

Behaving this way gave me the bizarre sense that I could control the outcome of everything in my life. I believed that being thin or skinny was the only way to achieve happiness and that I had to be relentlessly strict with myself. I would diet and diet until I just couldn't handle it anymore, and I then would give in to my cravings. Binge, binge, binge, and the cycle would start all over again.

I finally had to stop the insanity and take a deeper look at myself. I had to realize and accept that I was doing this shit to myself! Avoiding foods that I really love and forcing myself to eat foods that I couldn't stand was my version of insanity.

This part of my journey has been so eye opening. One of the many wonderful outcomes is that I'm not treating myself like a prisoner anymore. I don't like kale; it tastes like shit to me, and I'm super happy that I never have to eat it again! There are so many foods that are labeled *healthy* that taste absolutely disgusting to me.

Here is my gift to you—please pass it on: if there is a food you force yourself to eat because you think it's healthy and will keep your body small, but you hate the taste of it, or it doesn't make you or your body feel good, *stop eating it!*

There are so many foods in the world that make your body function optimally and taste amazing. It's quite a peaceful feeling knowing that food can make me feel my best, and that food can taste great.

You're Not Really Hungry

I was so hungry!

For me the most challenging part of my food awakening was confronting the dieting rules I believed, especially about hunger. There was a game I played over and over with myself, one that I could never win. The small amount of food that I allowed myself to eat during the day would never be enough, so by dinnertime I would get so hangry that I would start eating from one end of the kitchen and not stop until I got to the last piece of readily available food.

The question should never have been *Am I really hungry?* The only question should always be *What am I going to eat right now?*

I was constantly suffocating my real hunger with obnoxious diet rules, such as:

- Always drink sixteen ounces of water before eating.

- Wait twenty minutes and only then—and only if my stomach was still growling loud enough for people to hear—could I give in and eat something.

- I would force myself to eat only small meals, or not eat for hours and hours even if my stomach was begging me for food.

- I never let myself eat or drink anything after 7:00 p.m.

- I brushed my teeth after meals to cut the sweet cravings.

- During bouts of heavier restriction, I never ate bread or pasta.

- I didn't allow myself to eat before a workout.

- I couldn't lie down after I ate because that's how I would get fucking fat.

- I never, never ate anything immediately before going to bed.

As women, we are taught to believe all these completely harmful ways to control how much we eat. I know I chose to believe this crap, but it sounded perfectly legit at the time. Waking up and realizing all the things I did to myself to curb my appetite was abuse has changed my life. I remind myself every day that I am going to get hungry again later today and again tomorrow and the next day, and that's the way a healthy body works.

Why not just let eating food be *something I do* instead of *something that is done to me?* It's much more pleasant to exist this way.

I Didn't Fail the Diet—the Diet Failed Me

It is so important to understand the truth about dieting. I assure you diets are absolutely never going to work in the long term. Diets are designed to fail, so we must *keep dieting.* I really had to sit with that one. Every time I failed on a diet, I remember thinking that I was the real failure. *Why can't I get this weight off and keep it off?!* I would always spiral into the same thoughts of hopelessness. I felt like there was no way I could do this by myself. For years, I depended on everyone else to tell me how to lose weight. I was a little lazy, but mostly I was uneducated. I didn't know how my body worked and what it needed.

When you grow up having everything done for you, you think that's how the world works. I never took responsibility for my behaviors. I was repeatedly doing this to myself. I was the person who wasn't exercising consistently for weeks or months at a time and not fueling my body with the best foods possible.

My daily mantra was, "I'm so *fat,*" and I would say it to anyone who would happen to be around. My friends, my family, my coworkers. So why was I surprised or hurt when they would agree with me, or give me their advice on what to do with my body?

I realize now how exhausting it was being my friend. When I finally chose to wake up, I had a lot of forgiveness to ask for. To the ones who are still in my life, thank you, and I love you! They definitely have a much better friend in me these days. It was critical to the recovery of the daily disdain I had toward my body to realize that it was me who invited negative responses from people in my life. Only I could stop it.

Knowing finally that I can take care of myself and give my body everything it needs saved me from wasting another decade of my life. Being able to trust myself is priceless.

Rachel is my trainer and has been for six years. Her spunky and thoughtful approach to my training has made it easy to keep it up, and I don't intend to stop! Rachel is trustworthy, and it's so rewarding to see the changes in my body— how it looks and feels—which has only been possible through our consistency.

— Mary Ashton Y.

Chapter Two

Moving My Body
Then and Now

You have a mind and you have a body,
but in truth, you are Soul.

~Panache Desai

MOVEMENT IS HOW I SHOW MY BODY LOVE

It's time to share with you my lifelong relationship with exercise, movement, and working out. There are many names, but for me the word *movement* encompasses it all, mind, body, and spirit. When I find and practice a type of movement that I love, I feel an exhilarating difference in my body, as opposed to forcing my body to do something that doesn't feel good.

Specific types of movement have played a big role in my life, especially as an adult and as a fitness professional, but I've always loved moving my body. When I was a kid, I was lucky to have parents who let me try anything and everything related to sports and activities. I have loved all the different types of activities that I've been able to experience. Having the desire to move my body has never been my problem. When I was battling weight gain over and over again, it really came down to not understanding that my body needs consistency in this area, as well as finding the balance in both food and movement. As my body ages, the type of exercise I need to do has also changed and evolved.

I'll Try Anything Once

At every stage of my life, I can remember loving every type of movement that I was doing in the moment, and then I would get bored and move on to the next. I used to beat myself up about that, but now I accept that's just who I am. I love to try everything; some things stick and some don't.

My earliest memory was spending every waking moment swishing around in my grandparent's pool. My love for swimming started young. My family used to joke that I was a little fish, and they couldn't keep me out of the water. I was on a swim team for a time, swimming in meets every weekend. My best strokes were freestyle and the butterfly.

I dabbled in gymnastics, and even though I can still do a perfect cartwheel at forty-nine years old—thank you very much—it didn't really stick. I've taken every type of dance class available, and I loved performing. When I was ten years old, my mom remarried a wonderful man that I'm lucky to call Dad. He had been into snow skiing for most of his life, so we began skiing as a family. I enjoyed it, and I even tried downhill racing for one ski season.

Then I found the love of my life at that time—ice skating—and every other sport was cast aside. I was so in *love* with ice skating. I took it very seriously from sixth grade until my sophomore year in high school. I practiced every day after school, three times a week before school, and every weekend. I participated in local showcases and competitions; I even won first place once—that was so cool!—too bad I have no idea where my medal is.

Like most teenage girls, I found that high school was a completely different animal. I started making new friends and having a social life, and that became more important to me at the time. I gave up ice skating.

I never thought about doing sports professionally; I just knew they made me happy and that I loved moving my body. These activities always brought me so much joy. I never felt like it was a chore, and my parents never had to twist my arm to go to practice. It was something that made me feel good; it made me happy. I really enjoyed being able to experience each sport, but when I was done, I was done. This led to gaps in my movement habits, which led to weight gain.

Figuring It Out

After graduating high school in 1990, the last thing I wanted to do was go immediately to college. So, off I went to enjoy a gap year of fun in the sun on the island of Maui. During that year, I had significant weight loss because I was existing on SlimFast shakes. I was eighteen years old and working three different jobs to support my beach lifestyle, because Hawaii was expensive, even then.

After a year of having fun, I decided to come back to California, where I had been born and raised. This is where my love for Jazzercise began. My mom had been doing Jazzercise for quite some time and she loved it. After my return to the Mainland, I had no idea what my next step should be. My mom said, "Why don't you come to class with me?" I did, and the dancer in me instantly fell in love. I began taking weekly classes and soon could do all the routines just as well as the instructors.

In 1999, when I was twenty-six, I got married, and we moved to the Pacific Northwest. Not having a college degree, I started doing temp work, but it wasn't my joy in life. Then I landed a job as a receptionist for the company Bowflex, which was headquartered in Vancouver, Washington. If you don't remember, Bowflex was a huge manufacturer of the in-home gym apparatus that had its moment in the early 2000s. My desk was situated in the center of the massive call center, and I could hear the employees giving out exercise advice to customers who had just purchased a machine.

I remember thinking: *There's more to this; I want to help people with their workouts, too, not on the phone, but in person.* My marriage ended shortly after the move, and I decided not to go back to California but to attempt college again.

Even though I was now twenty-eight years old, when I found out that Portland Community College offered a one-year certification program in fitness technology, I immediately enrolled. School had always been a challenge for me, and I hadn't been a very good student in the past, but I really wanted to do this. I knew that being a personal trainer was what I was destined to do with my life.

The program was originally only a one-year certification, but when I was halfway through, it advanced into a two-year program, which meant I was would graduate with an actual degree (AAS). The academic part of school had always been hard for me, but this program was a combination of core academic and practical classes.

Because of the level of difficulty in those core classes, it took me a total of four years to complete that two-year program, but I refused to give up. I excelled in all my practical classes, and I was a natural teacher. I can honestly say I don't think I've ever connected with a person, place, or thing more than I have teaching fitness. Sorry to be cheesy, but it is my calling.

Becoming a Teacher

While I was in school, I earned money by teaching group exercise classes. I got certified as a Jazzercise instructor and ended up teaching from 2000 to 2007. I also started teaching aqua aerobics at a 24 Hour Fitness. I was making some new female friends in school, and it was so nice to know people in my life with common interests. When we weren't busy in class or studying, we spent our time trying all kinds of different fitness classes. I used to take a weekly hip-hop class with one of my girlfriends. I wasn't very good, but who cares; it was fun!

I found and fell in love with salsa dancing, and it gave me some of the best times of my adult life. The way I felt was very similar to the way I felt about ice skating. I put in the time to practice, and I got pretty good; I met some amazing lifelong friends, and our group performed locally. Salsa dancing was one of the few things I've done in my adult life that brought me completely out of my head; I was able to simply enjoy myself and just dance—without worrying about my body.

When I graduated in 2006, I stayed in the area for another year. I got a job at the beautiful Club Sport working as personal trainer. Club Sport is absolutely the single best job I've ever had in my entire personal training career, even after all these years and all the other gyms I have worked at. I look back on that experience with only the utmost fondness. I had some of the best mentors and gained valuable real-world experience that I've been able to apply throughout my career.

In 2007, I realized that I was ready to pursue my dream of moving to New York City to focus on my career as a certified personal trainer, and I've been here ever since.

EXERCISE IS ALWAYS THE ANSWER

Exercise is always the answer, right?

Wrong.

Even as a fitness professional, I am no stranger to having believed the latest and greatest new workout trend circling at the time; I have absolutely used exercise as a way to control my weight. You never have to go very far to find a special move or piece of equipment that promises to tone your triceps, melt your belly fat, strengthen and elongate your thighs, and lift your butt! I believed them all and you bet I tried them.

I realize now that I didn't have all the information that I needed to be successful. Results can absolutely be achieved with the right combination of movements and the right amount of calories and recovery time. I had to learn the difference between working out and exercising. My boyfriend loves to say, "It's called a workout for a reason: it's *work!*"

It's important to work all your muscles efficiently. Quality wins over quantity every time. Once I started doing that, I got results that I never knew my body was capable of. I work out smartly, I stretch, I get plenty of rest, and I eat enough food to replenish my body after a good workout.

After trying a multitude of forms of exercise and movement over the years, I've found that strength training works for me like nothing else ever has.

I absolutely love lifting weights. My body has responded so well to strength training, and I feel strong. I know I'm not 125 pounds anymore, but I really don't know how much I weigh. I really don't care about the number on the scale; I care about how I feel and how I'm able to move, pain free. My body was created to move, and we are all meant to move as well as we can for as long as we can.

Life as a Personal Trainer

I have been working as a fitness professional since 2000. I started my fitness career teaching group exercise. I've taught many different types of classes. During my last year of college, I took my ACE Personal Trainer exam and received my certification. I have spent the last fifteen years focusing solely on my work as a personal trainer. It is what I love to do.

I know I will always be in the fitness industry in some form for the rest of my life, but my new dream is to change the way the fitness industry responds to people with bigger bodies. How we fitness professionals treat our clients and each other is so important. It's time to accept that we come in various shapes and sizes, and people with bigger bodies don't need to be shamed or ridiculed into thinking they must go through extreme measures to become small.

We are all programmed to believe *no pain, no gain,* and that couldn't be more untrue. Eating food and moving our bodies should *feel good!* Our bodies process foods and movement differently. If someone in your life tells you otherwise, then it's time for them to go. I tease, but only slightly.

Believe in yourself and learn what's best for your body. It takes some time to figure that out. I've also had to be open to the reality that what is good for my body at forty won't necessarily be right for my body at sixty. I'm hoping to help create a movement to honor our differences, to encourage moving our bodies and eating the foods that make us feel our best at every age and every stage! No shame and no judgment.

Training My Clients

After twenty-plus years of personal training, I've learned how personal it really is. Even though most people come to me because they want to lose weight, it is my responsibility to train my clients safely and effectively. I have been on my own journey figuring out what works for me. I know I've pushed my beliefs onto my clients over the years. Even though I've gotten better as a trainer with every year, I've still given people workouts and meal plans that, upon reflection, weren't right for them. Now, I watch my clients' movement patterns and carefully tailor a program to fit their lifestyle and their needs.

The path to achieving results looks different for everyone. Not only did I have this epiphany about my body, my health, my eating, and my workouts, but I also had to realize that every single person I work with is going to go through these emotions and realizations as well. I need to be present and have empathy. I need to remind myself how long it took me to get to this place and be open enough to hear their stories without shoving my newfound knowledge down their throats.

I'm so happy to be free of yucky restriction and dieting rules, but some of the people I work with may not quite be there yet. I do promise to meet them where they are. I'll always remember that I was there, too, and that wasn't so long ago. It took me a long time to figure all this shit out, and I still do not have all the answers.

All I can do with this book is share with you that I have been there too. My eyes and my mind are finally open to my body's needs. I will be your ally and guide you through your own journey. As a professional personal trainer, it is important that I hear you, that I get to know you, and that I am able to be honest with you and myself.

Every Body Is Different

I've begun to put into practice having an open dialogue with my clients; it's important that I hear them and listen to their needs. Not all exercises work for everyone. If one isn't working, it is totally okay to throw it out! Just because an exercise is known to work a muscle effectively doesn't mean it's going to feel right for every one of my clients. It's perfectly acceptable to choose a different exercise that also works that specific muscle but feels good and comes more naturally to them.

When I work with my clients this way, it creates trust between us and promotes success for them. I used to wonder if I wasn't pushing my people hard enough, but I've realized practicing this kind of open dialogue has made me a better listener and has really broadened my perspective—not only for myself, but for my long-term clients who are getting much better results. It is possible to hear my clients' needs and respect where they are now and still train them effectively, challenge them, and help them achieve their goals. It is possible for workouts to be fun and still get results.

Some of my clients have stuck by me for years. I am even more grateful for the ones who have stuck by me during COVID-19. When I moved to New York City thirteen years ago, I began working with a client who has been by my side the entire time. I'm really proud of that.

I'M YOUR ADVOCATE, NOT YOUR ENABLER

I've recognized that enabling certain personalities doesn't do me—or them—any good in the long run. I've learned from my own experience that pushing someone to change a belief or personality trait before they are ready is completely detrimental to our working relationship. I want to enjoy all food and no longer restrict. I have found a way to enjoy exercise and do it consistently, but that doesn't mean that my clients are there yet.

I will always do my best to remember to put myself in your shoes and come from a place of love and nonjudgment. I know how long it took me to get here, and I will always appreciate my clients' boundaries. I will absolutely be an advocate for my present and future clients. I want you to feel good about your body now, no matter what size or shape your body is or will become. I will always support you. A trainer-client relationship is only valuable when it has trust and honesty. It is impossible to move forward if teamwork is not established.

Changing current habits can be hard, but I will remind you to be gentle with yourself. I can't do it for you. It's important to be responsible for yourself; you must accept that change starts with you. You must know that continuing to do things the way you've always done them isn't going to get you the results you want. My job is to help you feel confident in the gym so you can move on your own. I want you to be able to have the confidence to work out on your own. This doesn't have to be a struggle.

I've learned recently that it's a red flag if a client tells me that they won't work out without me; that situation can turn toxic very quickly. Throughout my career, I have seen plenty of other trainers give their clients outlandish workouts that the client couldn't possibly replicate on their own. This is unfortunately often intentional, and at what cost to that client? That is how people who are deconditioned get hurt.

I told myself early in my career that I was not going to train my clients that way. It is more important for my clients to feel confident and strong. I want you to appreciate, enjoy, and work hard during our sessions, but you should depend on yourself in the long run. I will always do my best to help my clients figure out the right recipe for them; we are a team, and we will work together until we find the right one.

I want to add that I can't fix what isn't broken because you, my friend, are not broken.

Moving My Body in My Forties

We all need to consider the effects of aging on our bodies. As I get older, certain exercises are just not going to feel good to my body anymore and may actually have adverse affects. Although exercise is very personal and very individualized, I have seen how moving my body in both the wrong and right way for me has impacted my body, and this is my experience.

I cannot tell you the number of times I snubbed my nose at certain aspects of movement routines, especially recovery. No matter how important exercise is, it does put stress on our bodies, and if we don't incorporate recovery, we will inevitably get hurt or experience pain. As I wrote this book, it was awesome to look back on all the different types of exercise that I've done: the swimming, dancing, and especially the skating. I will always have some kind of muscle memory for these activities. I love that I can still jump in a pool and glide through the water or dance with my boyfriend when a salsa song comes on our playlist.

As I age, I will have to adjust my movement routines to suit my body. I'm lifting weights on a weekly basis, and I need to stretch and foam roll and take rest days if I want to continue to do this when I'm ninety years old! I have gone through this interesting evolution of who I am as an exerciser. It has been a very rewarding experience, and I do know that where I am today is where I am supposed to be.

You Can't Pay Me to Do That Now

My body simply cannot do the same things at forty-nine that it could do when I was twenty, thirty, or even forty. In my twenties and thirties, I was always taking classes—from dance to boot camp. I could go to school all day, teach my classes, and then go take a 7:00 p.m. dance class. It's not a criticism to tell you that I absolutely cannot do that same kind of hustle at forty-nine; it's just a fact!

These days, I would rather get up early, do what I have to do, fit my workouts in between the hours of 9:00 a.m. and 11:00 a.m., be a total homebody in the evenings, and be in bed by ten o'clock! To be perfectly honest, I would rather walk through anything else than the doors of any kind of group exercise class; I just don't enjoy them anymore and my body just doesn't respond the same way it used to.

I now strength train; I love to lift weights. Strength training is the exception to my earlier comment. I will be able to do this for the rest of my life, but as the years go on, I will definitely need to adjust my program often to continue to get optimal results for my body's continually changing needs. From now on, I will always have to make time to stretch and rest my body. There is enough scientific information to back that up.

I tried so many different types of weight-training programs in the beginning, copying this person's or that person's workout. I found myself even more frustrated because I wasn't getting the same results that they were. I would be exhausted and irritable, or I would find myself thinking how much I hated it! Almost a year before the pandemic hit, I took my situation into my own hands and instead of doing what I always did, falling back into my old behaviors, I knew I had to advocate for myself.

I did some research and found that working my body in two parts, two times a week each, for a total of four days a week—with adequate rest in between—gives lasting results. So I designed a lower-body and upper-body program for myself. It consists of thoroughly working all my lower body muscle groups one day and my upper body muscle groups the next day, then a day of rest. I then repeat and have my weekends free! And I *love* it!

I really started to see changes in my muscle development, and my body composition changed. This program also makes me feel that I'm able to have a life outside of the gym. I have three other days a week to do whatever the hell I want, and I don't even have to think about seeing the inside of a gym on those days. I no longer beat myself up or feel guilty for skipping a workout to hang out with a friend or my boyfriend, or spend hours roaming the aisles of Target; it's my day off from the gym and I can do whatever I want.

Of course, in a perfect world, life would never dare get in the way of my workout schedule. Alas, it does; in that case, I can rearrange my days for that week or simply say *fuck it* and get in three workouts instead of four. It's okay. I've realized that long-term consistency is the key.

I finally like the type of exercise I'm doing. Here's a good tip for people who also struggle with consistency with your workouts: It's important to find something that you enjoy but also leaves you feeling good all over, because if you don't like your workouts, you won't stick with them for the long term. My thinking has evolved; with that evolution has come the acceptance that moving my body is something I will do every week for the rest of my life. It has become a part of my essence, and I am able to relax.

Rest and Recovery Is the New Black

As I evolved to understand how to treat my body and its constantly changing needs, I had to learn to listen to it.

When it came to eating, I realized my body knows when it is hungry. In the same way, my body also knows when it's drained of all energy and needs to rest.

Learning how to pay attention to my body's signals is a wonderful beginning, but actually acting on those signals is another thing. I've had to recognize my body telling me I just can't work out today because of minor pains or muscle soreness or just having drained energy throughout my body. I pay attention and I give myself permission, without guilt, to rest an extra day.

Another interesting thing that I have learned on my journey is there are some unexpected benefits of adding stretching and foam rolling into my exercise routine.

Previously, I would often be in pain and would sometimes experience bloating, which is caused by fluids getting trapped in between my muscles. For a long time, I wasn't doing recovery after my workouts, because—let's face it—I don't have time! But I was always in some kind of pain, my hips mostly. I developed *piriformis syndrome.*

The piriformis is a muscle with a pear-like shape located in your buttocks. It extends from the bottom of your spine to the top of your thigh. Tenseness and tightness of this muscle can induce an involuntary spasm. When this muscle tightens, it can also compress against the sciatic nerve, which passes next to the piriformis. The sciatic nerve is the biggest single nerve in the human body. This nerve is a vital connector between the spinal cord and the leg and foot muscles. If the piriformis spasm compresses the sciatic nerve, this can cause shooting pain, tingling, or numbness anywhere from the hip to the lower leg or foot.[1]

Pain is our body's way of asking for help, and I had no choice but to listen. Even when I don't want to, I remind myself that stretching in tandem with strength training is critical to my body's well-being and with living a life of mobility. Learning how to help myself through these bouts of pain was empowering.

I also realized that if I didn't stretch after every workout, and sometimes in between, I was going to begin to resent my workouts. This would make me stop and then the cycle would repeat itself. Knowing that I am taking care of my body, mind, and spirit has changed everything for me. Even though I'm in a bigger body than I was a few years ago, and now—during COVID—even a few months ago, I still feel so much better from head to toe today because I know how to treat my body with care.

---

1 Facty Staff. "10 Symptoms of Piriformis Syndrome." February 21, 2020. facty.com/ailments/body/10-symptoms-of-piriformis-syndrome/

> *Rachel and I have been working together for fourteen years. We have a special bond, and I trust her to take care of me and my body's needs. There isn't another person who gets my wacky sense of humor like Rachel does.*
>
> — Hugh T.

Chapter Three

Self-Love Started at Forty

When I let go of the girl I was pretending to be and fell in love with the real me, I found the key that unlocked the cage and set me free.

~ Hannah Blum

MY WAKEUP CALL AT FORTY

I might have mentioned to you how I haven't felt comfortable in my own skin for most of my life. I know I've always had a negative relationship with my body, but after doing the emotional work, I get how my emotional well-being is tied to my feelings about my body. I realize now that I never knew who I really was. I have a much better understanding of how I feel and how I treat myself on the outside affects how my body responds on the inside.

When I turned forty years old, I experienced an awakening unlike anything before or since. Although it is still a process, my forties have been the best decade of my life so far.

Putting the Pieces Back Together

As my fortieth birthday was quickly approaching, I was exhausted living as the person I'd been for so long. So many things began to happen at once and I believe the universe was throwing multiple signs at me to get my attention so it could say to me, "*Girl*, it's time to snap out of this!"

I felt completely drained of all energy, good and bad. I just felt weary from head to toe. I began taking steps to learn about the forty-year-old woman I was soon to be, to align myself with the person that I was really meant to be. I read some amazing books that really opened my heart. I started listening to love songs in a different way. I realized that if you apply song lyrics to yourself, they can become quite a powerful tool for reinforcing self-love.

Each day I urged myself to push through the pain and deal with my past. I cleansed myself by doing a lot of work and could feel myself unclenching from years of stress. There were days when it got really hard, but I refused to give up on myself this time.

I allowed Rachel—the little girl who didn't trust anyone but wanted to be loved so badly—to feel the pain and realize that I, Rachel the adult, was capable of being her own support system. From that point on, I was was going to protect her and unconditionally love her and remind her that she is beautiful and worthy.

I felt my spirit getting stronger, and all the things I ever wanted began entering my life. I treated myself with love, kindness, and acceptance. I learned how to self-soothe myself emotionally, which was something I had been incapable of before. I chose—and continue to choose—to stay conscious of how I look at life and the way it affects not only me, but also other people.

I realize that life isn't about not making any mistakes; it is about how we learn and grow from those mistakes. I recognize that this is a lifelong process, but it's nice to have a peaceful existence most of the time. I don't take for granted how beautiful life is anymore. I am so grateful for that.

Standing on My Own

The first week after turning forty years old, a day came that was so special—I had an ethereal life-changing experience that I will never forget. I remember it so vividly! I usually spent my time between clients at the gym. Between the morning rush and the lunch rush, there was always that midmorning lull that was nice and quiet.

Normally, I would use that time to work out, but this day was clearly meant for a heart- opening experience. Without any provocation, I wandered into the group exercise room. It was empty and all the lights were turned off. I stepped inside where the walls were all mirrored except for the door leading in and out.

I chose a spot in the deepest corner of the room and sat down on the floor. I could see a light surrounding my reflection. In that moment, I could feel something washing over me. I wasn't afraid; I felt like I was weightless. I looked at my reflection—really looked—and I could see into my soul. I saw a beautiful, glowing woman looking back at me; she *was* me.

I began to sob so hard my body shook, and there was absolutely no sound from my crying. I didn't even feel like I had to blink; tears were just pouring down my cheeks nonstop. I kept looking at this beautiful woman in the mirror. We were both crying and then we both started to laugh. Everything that had ever been done to me or that I had done to myself was leaving my body that day; I was being freed from of all the pain and hurt. It was the most beautiful experience that I have ever had in my life.

I was seeing Rachel, the woman, for the first time. I continued both crying and laughing simultaneously, but the knowledge that was filling up inside me was that I had always been the person that I had wanted to be. During all the years I spent thinking I was the opposite of who I really was, I was beautiful.

I have always been beautiful, I was always kind, I was always capable, and I was always good enough.

Honestly, I floated out of that room that day. I know that experience changed me forever.

I'm Still Learning

Even after all the work I've done on myself and continue to do, the hardest part is dealing with my emotional response to seeing my reflection or physically feeling the weight on my body. On those days, when my instinct is to be cruel, I remind myself to be gentle and loving to myself. It takes a certain level of awareness to keep those old responses from emerging. One of the most valuable lessons I have had to learn and accept was that, having spoken negatively about my body every day for the better part of forty-nine years, it would be ludicrous to expect that would go away overnight.

Now I must use tools, sometimes multiple times day, to help me speak to myself with kindness; that is the only way I'm truly going to heal. My goal is to have a full twenty-four hours in which I don't have one negative thought about my body in any way. I can't wait for that day!

After that, I'll keep setting new goals. After one full day of no negative thoughts, I'll go for two straight days, then an entire week, maybe a month! Right now, that seems out of my reach, but I will keep doing my best. In the meantime, I will continue to be gentle with myself. Every day, I tell my body *I love you*; I tell my body *thank you*; sometimes I just tell my body *you're okay*.

FORTY IS FABULOUS

Forty is fabulous! Super cheesy, I know—but for me this is so true! I have learned so much, and I have had the best decade of my life so far. The past ten years have been a learning experience unlike anything I could've had anywhere other than New York City. I was able to learn how to break all the cycles that hindered me, to become a self-sufficient adult who could deal with situations on my own, to become a woman who could take care of my responsibilities. I learned that true love had to start with me loving myself more than anyone or anything. My body has undergone a truly extraordinary overhaul.

Negative Self-Talk Is an ASSHOLE

I had to address negative self-talk—hard core! I was the one on a daily basis ripping myself to shreds verbally in reference to my body. I had to become conscious of the things I was saying out loud about my body and realize that they were only reinforcing the way my body responded. I would single out a body part and relentlessly pick it apart; nothing was off limits. My man shoulders, my fat gut, my triple chins, my back fat, or my non-existent ass!

Taking on the negative self-talk has been challenging. It felt so strange in the beginning to change the way I spoke about myself. At first, all I could do when my inner chatter began spouting off this and that about my body was to counteract those ingrained responses with new and loving responses.

Sometimes I would literally have to stop myself from saying the thought that was already forming on my lips. Now I can say to myself: *I am beautiful; I am not fat; I know I am in a bigger body now but that doesn't make me unworthy of love; my body is whole the way it is now and forever.*

I still must do this when those thoughts enter my mind; I know this is going to take time. I would like to add that it's inevitable that negative talk will slip out from time to time, and it doesn't mean that all the strides I've made are lost. I just keep reminding myself four decades is a long time, and this isn't going to stop overnight.

Choosing to Be Happy

A short time after my fortieth birthday I really wanted to know who I was. I had spent most of my life cutting people out any time things got uncomfortable, so I didn't really trust people. That makes it very hard to have meaningful relationships. I knew I was going to have to work at becoming a whole person. I chose to clean up my past and reconnect with my estranged friends and a few family members.

My biological father was one of those people. It was such a beautiful experience because I was able to forgive and stay open. During one of our early conversations, he told me that I was always such a happy kid, and that took me aback since I spent most of my adult life being unhappy. I wanted to learn how to authentically become my own best friend and continue being happy. I spent time discovering who I was by learning how to be alone.

Living in New York City, you are never alone; there are always people on the street, in front of you, behind you, to the left and to the right of you, but it can also seem like the loneliest place on earth. I had to sit in my discomfort, and the only way I was going to know *who the hell I was* was to go and live my life. I stopped waiting around for someone else to do things with; I just started taking myself on dates. I was having a great time! I realized that I was a pretty cool lady and a lot of fun to hang out with.

I was beginning to experience life differently and I was enjoying myself. I trusted myself more and more; being alone wasn't causing me anxiety the way it used to. I felt like I could start dating again and I could start having deeper and more whole relationships with men, my friends, and my family. I have made a conscious choice to never lose sight of that part of me; I still absolutely value my alone time.

Trusting Myself

My body has put up with a lot of shit over the years, and it still kept me alive. I know it will need time to heal from all the dieting and restricting. I owe my body so much gratitude, and I plan on thanking it every day moving forward.

I want to reiterate my message that trusting your body completely doesn't mean that you don't need to do your part to take care of it. Now that food is not my enemy, I know that my body will tell me what I need through cravings; sometimes I need broccoli, or sometimes my body really wants pineapple, or I just need a scrumptious doughnut and I need it now! Over the past few years since my last big diet, I really have learned what kind of foods my body best responds to. The few things my body says *no thank you* to are those that give me discomfort or cause bloating.

How my body looks on the outside starts with the way it is treated on the inside. It is phenomenal what our bodies are capable of and how much they actually put up with. Letting go and paying attention to what my body needs has helped me to loosen the reins a little bit more each day and really trust my body. I know it only wants the best for me.

My Reflection

For years, the most painful thing about my body was seeing my reflection in a window or a picture of myself. I would hatefully pick my body apart from head to toe. I remember countless occasions when I would look at a picture of myself and be mortified at the vision of my body because I thought I looked so fat! I never wanted to take a picture from the neck down, and I would always try to manage group photos with my girlfriends so I could hide in the back. It was especially hard if I saw a thin photo of myself after another weight gain; I thought the sky was falling. But walking by a store window might have been even worse because my reaction was so hateful. I would instantly say to myself how fat I looked and then it would consume me, sometimes to the point where I couldn't enjoy myself for the rest of the day.

These reactions to seeing my reflection or seeing myself in a picture are visceral. I know you have had these same feelings. I really wanted to put the joy back into my life and stop missing out on beautiful memories and experiences because I don't want to see how my body looks. Now when I see a picture of myself that at first I think is unflattering, or I pass by a window and my initial response is to be hurtful, I ask myself to look at my reflection again but with grateful eyes instead of judgment. I remind myself how lucky I am that I'm able to wake up every morning and I get up and move my body. That one picture doesn't tell my whole story.

It will be a wonderful occasion when I have no reaction at all to seeing myself in a picture, or when I can walk by a store window and not even see my body but just the beautiful display inside. Until that dream is a reality, I will continue to tell myself that I'm okay, that I am beautiful today. I will continue to hold my own hand through this process and remind myself that my body is my best friend, and it is perfect right now.

Rachel possesses a passion for what she believes in and wants to share the knowledge she has gained through her experiences with the rest of the world. That is a characteristic that not all can claim. To know Ms. Lavin is to absolutely love her.

— Samaneh Biria H.

Chapter Four

My Body, My Business

What other people think of me is none of my business.
~ attributed to Eleanor Roosevelt

IT'S MY BODY

This chapter is meant to share with you how much of my energy I was spending on living my life for everyone else. My mind was always consumed with negative thoughts about my body. My time was spent ignoring my body and the things that it needed from me. I am still learning how not to do this.

My body has always known what it needs and how to ask for it. I just wasn't listening until now.

It's None of My Business:

One extremely valuable lesson I had to learn during this life-altering journey was that I had to stop asking everyone else how my body looked. I spent my entire life looking outside myself for approval. I continuously invited chaos into my world because of other people's opinions or ideas of what my body should look like.

I know I'm not alone in this. Most of us have experienced this horrendous cycle. It's time to stop this shit and get our power back! I realized that if I was really going to be able to love my body at any size, I needed to be the only one with any thoughts on the matter about my body!

In the past, I allowed people in various stages of my life to treat me poorly, but that's because I didn't have enough self-respect to love myself. It's terrible that I accepted that type of abuse and negativity from other people. I often wonder if I hadn't degraded my body the way I did for so many years—regarding how I looked or how much space my body took up—would anyone else have?

I always believed that everyone else was thinking negatively about my body, so I would often blurt out statements like "I know I'm fat!" or "Don't freak out when you see me because I've gained so much weight." I just assumed that's what they were thinking about my body. The hard truth is that even if they are, it is absolutely none of my business what anyone else thinks about the size or shape of my body. Even if I gain weight or lose weight, I don't need to be shamed or validated by anyone.

Now that my body has changed again, I've tested this theory in the past few months. Instead of saying a word to anyone, I'm just observing how people respond to me not reacting to my body. I'm happy to report that I'm still recognizable on the street even with a mask on, my boyfriend still grabs my butt every day, and when I'm having fun quarantine FaceTime chats with my girlfriends, not one of them has made any comments about my body or my weight gain. We just have great talks and laugh our asses off!

During this time, I have been able to see my interactions with other people much more clearly. I had to learn to understand that I was my own worst enemy and people were responding to my negative energy. Now that I have chosen to stop the madness and be my own cheerleader, I no longer worry about anyone taking my power from me ever again.

I Didn't Ask You

I absolutely do not talk negatively about my body to anyone anymore. This has been so critical to healing the relationship with my body. All the years that I spent putting myself down to other people only created more distance between loving my body and myself. I allowed other people's criticism and opinions about my body to crush me. I believed *them* instead of *myself*!

The things I was told to do with my body and how I should make it smaller overshadowed my desire to be comfortable in my own skin and figure out for myself what my body needed. It's true that when you constantly look outside yourself for advice about your body—what to eat, when to eat, how to work out—you don't stop and wonder whether what works for someone else will work the same way for you.

I just didn't want or know how to reclaim my body on my own. When I decided that I was going to stop listening to outside influences and really take care of myself, I would also have to deal with all the feelings by myself.

When I'm having a hard time being kind to myself and the weight on my body becomes momentarily unbearable, I remind myself why I'm doing this:

- To be free
- To trust my body and myself
- To stay happy

My aim is to finally have a day, a week, a month, and even a year where not one thing about my body is negative. Right now, it's only seconds or minutes at a time, but I keep those negative feeling to myself, and I don't involve anyone anymore. I don't do this to suffer; I do it because it's crucial to my recovery.

If you recall, earlier I shared with you how the Rachel who used to exist was incapable of taking care of herself in any way. I always needed people to do everything for me, and that wasn't going work this time. I chose to believe what was true all along—that I was always enough. For me, this is what I had to do, especially during this time. I had to trust only myself about my body and how it looks and feels.

My Body Knows What It Needs

Along this amazing adventure, I had to stop fighting with myself and truly accept that my body is smart as hell. It knows what it needs and when it needs it. My responsibility is to provide those things—such as food, rest, and movement. The one signal I often ignored was allowing myself to get too hungry. I really believed that I could outsmart my hunger. Wrong!

I have believed in so many diet myths my whole life. The things I've done are nothing I would repeat now. During all those years of dieting, restricting, and bingeing, I never thought to ask myself: *Why don't you just eat when you get hungry?*

I made something that is so natural and easy so difficult. The truth is simple. For years, I fought tooth and nail against what my body is innately created to do. I'm grateful that I have been able to break those lifelong patterns of believing that my hunger wasn't real. I also know how much of my life those beliefs stole from me. Thankfully, my heart and my mind are open, and I can throw out all the bullshit that I was taught. I can trust my body without any doubt in my mind that it knows what to do, that its only task is to keep me alive, and it's doing a wonderful job!

Thank you, Body!

PUTTING MY BODY THROUGH THE RINGER

I have realized throughout this process that loving my body takes work. It's not an exaggeration to say that, for so long, I hated my body and I hated how I saw my body. That is my truth. Instead of taking action and advocating for my health and well-being, I would just wish that I could love my body. Many times during my life, I would make futile attempts toward improving my health, but because I wasn't armed with the right information or self-awareness, it would end up being a very half-assed and short-lived change.

The truth is that I did not appreciate my body and everything it does for me every second of every day. It is extraordinary and beautiful all on its own! I couldn't be more grateful that I'm aware of this now. I recognize how special that is. I will never take it for granted again. Although the first half of my life was spent hating my body, I get to spend the second half loving it. I had to change hateful thoughts and actions to loving ones.

Changing my mindset was and is crucial to the success of loving my body and myself. I can't just wish for it. I have to work for it.

Overnight Success?

I really had to let go of the idea of instant gratification with reference to my body. The numerous declarations I would make and the major lifestyle changes I attempted would be so short-lived because nothing would happen overnight, and I would give up.

I'm sure you have had thoughts like I did: *Where the hell did this weight come from and conversely, dammit, why is it taking forever to get it off?*

Truth bomb: They both happen over time. It's always important to recognize that real change takes time.

My body has gone through so many gains and losses, I found myself wondering how it would respond to just letting it be—while simply providing daily care for it. Movement, nourishment, and rest are the three staples that I do for myself daily.

That also means accepting that every day I need to:

- Nourish my body with good food
- Move my body with the right type of exercise
- Apply proper recovery and plenty of rest

The agony of what I put my body through is over. I want that for you too. Say goodbye to all those unrealistic expectations of how you think you need to treat your body. Do your best to be present and loving. Just be.

I Can Eat Anything?

Yes, I can eat anything. This is part of the process that I embrace daily, to relinquish all control, giving in to the idea that I should love my body at any size. I want to believe with my whole heart that my body only wants to take care of me and be its best self, even if I take up more space than I used to, even if I'm in a bigger body. That is scary as hell!

The decade of my forties has been a constant growing period. In 2019, I took another hard look at how I was still restricting foods because they were going to lead to weight gain. But that metaphorical light bulb was blinding me; I really wanted a healthier relationship with *all* foods. My caloric needs were changing because my workouts had changed. My lower-body/upper-body split was awesome, but I could feel my body changing and I started to worry.

Of course, my first thought was that I needed to restrict, but a book with a catchy title piqued my interest. In *The F*ck It Diet: Eating Should Be Easy,* Caroline Dooner writes about intuitive eating and how to throw out diet culture completely. I was astounded that this was a thing! I read a few more books on the topic and began following women just like me on social media. I began saying *yes* instead of *no* to the foods that I never allowed myself to eat.

It was daunting putting that first bite of something that I had otherwise restricted into my body, but my desire for complete freedom from the fear of gaining weight, food rules, and restrictive beliefs was guiding me now. There was no way I could lead my clients down this path of accepting their body at any size and stopping the practice of restricting foods if I wasn't willing to do it for myself.

I didn't think it was possible to enjoy my food the way that I do now. It has taken time to adapt to allowing myself freedom to eat while taking good care of myself. It has taken time to accept and love my body. I would love to be able to tell you how long it's going to take for you to love your body at any size, but I can't; everyone's journey is going to be different and very personal. I would like to ask you to be patient with yourself and just enjoy the process.

Shit Happens

I know my latest strength-training program was really working for me. Training four days a week and eating the foods that make me happy and satisfied had quelled the negative inner chatter for the most part. My clothes were still feeling good on my changing body, and I was out in the city moving around from client to client, enjoying my New York City life.

Then March 17, 2020, happened and the COVID-19 pandemic changed our lives completely. My entire routine changed overnight, and as the days and months of this quarantine continue, I've had to adapt and create a new routine for myself. This has been hard. My body has changed during 2020 and that change has given me more perspective. The way I lived my life before and what I had done to my body over the years was not healthy or whole behavior.

But now, more than ever, I realize I wasn't born so I could hate my body or my life. I was put on this Earth to learn and grow. It is never too late, and I will never be too old to realize that I'm good enough. I have always been good enough. My goal moving forward as a personal trainer and the author of this book is to share my experience with my clients and with you, to help others see that it is possible to love your body at any age or at any size.

Please gently remind yourself that it takes time to change these habits that weigh you down mentally, emotionally, and even physically. Not even a pandemic can take the desire to love your body from you, even after all the changes we went through this year. Do your best to stay open. Open up your heart and your mind and let go of beliefs that you have used to control your weight up until now. The reality is that these fears will only keep us in lockdown and keep us from living our best lives.

HOPE: HONESTY, OPTIMISM, PEACE, ENTHUSIASM

Now that I have finally written this book, I've been able to see the bigger picture. As much as I appreciate you reading my story and realizing how all along you weren't alone, it's not just about me or you. It's time to lift up the next generation and the next and the next after that. Let's continue to learn that our bodies are as individual as our personalities, and they don't have to fit inside the same unimaginative stigmas they always have.

It's time for real change. Every single human deserves to take up all their space in this world and do it with peace of mind that they won't be hurt physically or emotionally. I have realized during this process how much time and energy I have given to only my body. Before I started this new way of taking care of myself, I believed that nothing could change, that this was the life I would always have, that I was always going to struggle with hating my body. But I found hope, and that is so powerful! Hope is what I want to share with you.

Apologizing to My Body

I want to apologize to my body here in front of you:

Dear Body,

I'm so, so sorry. Even when I didn't have faith in you, you took care of me, and I am so grateful for you. I love you. I promise you that I will continue to do my best for the rest of my life and take care of you in the way that you deserve.

After this experience, it doesn't surprise me that a simple message like loving my body at any size had been lost on me for decades. I only had to hear it over and over again a gazillion times before it finally sank in, and I was ready to take action. But that's how a lot of of us are. It takes a million misses to get to the one bull's eye.

My book isn't meant to tell you to hurry the fuck up and just love yourself! I know that's impossible, and it's not going to be easy breezy; it's not supposed to be. Digging deep and figuring out why you've hated your body takes time, tears, and healing. Maybe my story is different from your story, maybe not, but love is universal. If you can start to apply it to yourself, you're going to find the freedom that you've always longed for.

I have accepted that I had to forgive myself for everything that I put my body through. I had to tell myself and my body I was sorry for not believing what it was capable of all along. I apologized for not respecting myself, for hiding myself away from the world, for not being honest with myself, not trusting myself, and not loving myself.

I know that's a lot, but when you come out the other side, it is so damn bright and beautiful here. Please come join me.

Rachel is equally hilarious, honest, and whole-hearted. She's got an uncanny ability to shine a light on the path forward in a way that is disarming, no bullshit, and incredibly supportive. Rachel's clients are highly successful because she walks her talk. She has done the work personally on every level, which allows her to provide coaching that is clear, targeted, and results driven.

— Debra D.

Chapter Five

Becoming Whole

We are not meant to be perfect; we're meant to be whole.
~ Jane Fonda

FOOD ISN'T A DIRTY WORD

In this final chapter, I want to tell you how important it was for me to heal my relationship, not just with my body, but my entire being. I've told you umpteen times throughout this book that I needed to realize how my negative relationship with food was affecting my happiness, my weight, my attitude, the way I trained my clients, and the way that I lived my everyday life. However, the entire process is bigger than just eating all foods and no longer restricting. It is accepting that food isn't here to hurt me.

I had to accept that food was my friend. I respect my body, and it's okay to nourish it with food. I chose to love my body enough to not care what other people thought of the type of foods that I eat. I was so tired of fighting with myself. Living every day with all these diet rules and regulations depleted me, and I wasn't going to allow them to take up the same amount of space in my brain or my time or energy anymore.

I No Longer Say, "I Can't Eat That"

For years, I would regularly declare—

I CAN'T EAT THAT!

—until I realized that it came from my fear of being fat. Being fat scared the shit out of me for so long!

My mind was always dominated by the foods I wasn't allowed to have. When I would sneak one of my so-called bad foods, the immediate afterthought was: *This is going to make me fat!* I had been living such an unfulfilled life by repeatedly telling myself: *I can't eat that or I don't eat that.*

Doughnuts are a perfect example. My uncle had taken me to Winchell's Donut House—it's a California thing—since I was a little girl. There was never any shame attached to it. I just ordered my vanilla cake doughnut with rainbow sprinkles and went on about my day. At some point, someone told me doughnuts were fattening and bad for me, so out of my life they went for years and years.

There were countless foods that I thought about this way, believing one bite of a *bad* food on a Sunday was going to show up on my body on Monday. During this journey, I realized all my beliefs were a load of crap! A big ole cake doughnut was the first *bad* food I allowed myself when I decided to stop restricting foods. I savored every bite, and really allowed myself to enjoy my yummy doughnut. The reality is that not any one food or food group is going to make me fat.

Just Don't Keep It in the House

We must talk about bingeing. Dieting and bingeing are best frenemies; they are inseparable. And they are powerful. It didn't matter how much self-control I exuded. It didn't matter if I dieted for months straight and never touched one crumb of food that was going to derail my weight loss. Those two would inevitably conspire against me and they would break me.

I would end up eating the entire bag of chips instead of the seven chips that the serving size allowed me on the back of the bag. Or I would eat the entire candy bar, not just half. I would really get pissed off at myself for being physically weak and then I would mentally and emotionally punish myself.

Sometimes I could get right back on my diet and pretend that eating the entire package of mini powdered doughnuts didn't happen. But then there were times when the binge might last a few days or weeks and I would eat all the foods that were on my naughty list.

Do you see the correlation?

The solution was, of course, another diet rule that we have all heard and that you may be continuing to live by. It's the rule called:

Just don't have it in the house!

If it's not in my kitchen then I can't eat it, right? It sounds logical, but what happens when I'm not in the safety of my calorie-fest-free home?

Unfortunately, when we go out into the world, those *bad* foods are everywhere. Because of this, I isolated myself a lot. I wouldn't go out to dinner with my friends or put myself in social situations where snack tables would be around. When my friends could finally convince me to go with them, I would have to announce emphatically, "I'm on a diet, so don't get dessert!"

I could give you a trillion examples of dieting and bingeing, but I'd rather tell you some happy news: it's all bullshit. I had to dispel yet another diet/food lie that I believed in so fervently. Bingeing was inevitable because I was restricting foods and not allowing myself to just be happy and have a damn doughnut or whatever I deemed *bad* at the moment.

I wasn't bingeing because I am a weak or bad person. In this life, we are meant to be happy and whole. Having access to *all* foods without restriction takes away the *need* to binge. I now keep chocolate in my home, and I have a piece or two every day. That makes me happy. When I'm craving something else like a cookie, a doughnut, or a slice of chocolate cake, I order that shit from Postmates—a home grocery delivery service—and enjoy every single bite. I no longer punish myself or allow myself to fixate on the thought that someone else is going to judge me or shame me. I no longer punish myself for—this is a big one!—doing the one thing I'm put on this earth to do: smile and be happy! I promise you that since I stopped restricting any food, I have not binged on anything.

Signals and Set Points

Since reintroducing foods that I had been restricting, I'm more aware of how they make my body feel overall. I do have to be very honest with you; I do believe that some foods don't react well with my body, and it lets me know by farting or painfully bloating. If this happens to you, know you're not alone here either.

Our bodies are smart. It's important to understand the signals that our bodies give us. Those signals are designed to let us know when our bodies are not okay or when they couldn't be happier with the foods that we put into them. When I have eaten something that my body doesn't react well to, I remind myself this pain is temporary, and there are things I can do to help myself. I don't have to eat that particular food again. On the other hand, when I eat a food that my body responds well to, I can feel my energy soaring; I feel like I can fly!

I want to spread this message strongly: I don't have to eat foods that just don't taste good to me. It doesn't matter how healthy they are supposed to be. Some foods in the healthy category do not react well with our bodies, but we keep eating them, and we keep suffering. I had to reevaluate the foods that I ate and really pay attention to how my body was reacting to these foods.

A fun fact I'm sure by now you get is that I love doughnuts. However, I have found that although my body can comfortably digest a cake doughnut, it can't be bothered with a yeast doughnut. This is an example of something I have been able to learn by eating and paying attention to how my body responds.

I know I have done some crazy shit to my body, from dieting to bingeing to over- or under-exercising; I have challenged and confused my body over the years. I have accepted that my body is not against me, that it wants to keep me healthy and moving for as long as possible. I understand now that I can trust it to take care of me, and I need to take care of it.

My body has a *set point*.[2] Even during my countless weight loss ups and downs, my body tends to settle at one hundred

2 Set Point Theory states that our bodies have a preset weight baseline hardwired into our DNA. According to this theory, our weight, and how much it may change from that set point, might be limited. The theory says some of us have higher weight set points than others, and our bodies fight to stay within these ranges (Ghoshal, Malini. "What You Need to Know About Set Point Theory." *Healthline*. 19 March

and fifty pounds. A very interesting discovery I have made regarding my body's set point is that although it may stay at one hundred and fifty pounds, consistently doing a strength-training routine and working my body effectively and efficiently caused the shape of my body to change. I have muscle definition and I feel strong.

BMI IS BULLSHIT

The only aspect of my job as a personal trainer that I despised from day one was doing the *assessment*. This was a battery of tests that I had to perform on a potential client's body. It included a *skin fold test*, which would tell them how much body fat they carried, an inventory on their food intake, and a BMI (*body mass index*)[3] calculation.

In my opinion, this assessment is only done to make a person feel even worse about themselves, and to make them believe they are fucked and can't do this alone. The inventory on food intake was invasive and all the tests represented an antiquated aspect of personal training. I honestly never did

---

2020. healthline.com/health/set-point-theory)
3 The BMI was introduced in the early 19th century by a Belgian named Lambert Adolphe Jacques Quetelet. He was a mathematician, not a physician. He produced the formula to give a quick and easy way to measure the degree of obesity of the general population to assist the government in allocating resources. In other words, it is a 200-year-old hack. (Devlin, Kevin. "Top 10 Reasons Why the BMI Is Bogus."*npr.* 04 July 2009. npr.org/templates/story/story.php?storyId=106268439

the body fat test on my clients in the real world. I stopped that once I graduated from college. I always felt like I was body-shaming people and if anyone knew that feeling, it was me.

BMI is used inappropriately to scare the shit out of you, so you think that you are obese and a walking bag of disease. We have lived in a world where it has been acceptable to call someone obese because they don't fit into the right category on a chart that was created in the 1800s. It divides a person's weight by height to determine if they are carrying a healthy amount of weight. I know I'm skipping over the science-y part, but my message is this: I'm not going to believe that some chart that's never met me gets to tell me what my damn body should look like or how much I should weigh!

The Scale Is a C-U-NextTuesday

Even though this part is very personal and stems from my experience, I'm sure you will be able to relate. The scale has played two very distinct roles in my life. I'll begin with the good because that won't take very long. During my last fifty-pound weight loss, I was so excited to see the number on the scale go lower and lower every day. It was awesome! Every single morning, I would wake up, make sure to pee, then strip off all my clothes and wait for the flashing number to stop on . . .

Now for the way I really experienced the scale for most of my life. Logically, scales exist to tell you how much you weigh in that given moment, which—for someone like me who has lost weight and gained weight, you know the story, *a lot!*—made me feel like a complete and utter failure. Seeing the number on the scale go up, even if it was only half a pound, I would beat the shit out of myself. I would get angry and hate my body even more—if that was possible. I would weigh myself five times in a row to see if something was wrong with that C-U-NextTuesday. I would hit the reset button and pray that the lower number I had seen yesterday reappeared. I would be so disappointed in myself all day. Of course, I would restrict my food intake, ignoring my hunger, which would only add more stress to my already poor underfed body. That cycle would repeat itself, and I would only see the number go up.

I believed I was doing everything right, but nope, that little C-U-NextTuesday had its own plan. Throughout my life, I have had many heart-stopping moments of stepping on the scale and having a large number flash back, taunting me: 150, 155, 160, and of course, the infamous 170.

I honestly have no idea what the number is now, and I'm going to keep it that way. Weighing myself daily is definitely not something that works for me. I have realized that, for someone like me who was putting their entire value as a person in that number, weighing myself daily was not going to be a part of my recovery.

The feelings attached to the number on a scale don't fall in line with the way I feel about my body now, so I threw my scale away, and I will *never* own one again. And just as simple as that, there is peace in my heart and in my life knowing that I never have to be told by a little computer if my body weight is acceptable, because I already know that I am.

I do have to openly apologize to my clients. I know I have asked you to weigh yourself during the time that you were working with me, and I'm so sorry. I was doing what I believed in at the time, and now I know better.

Super-quick sidenote: I've recently learned that it is your choice to be weighed at a doctor's office, and you can say a polite *no thank you*. I have put this into practice, and it worked. I also have a response ready if they ask me why, and you can feel free to use it: "I'm recovering from a negative body image and seeing the number on the scale will only set me back."

An afterthought about the scale otherwise known as the C-U-NextTuesday. If you are a daily weigh-er like I was and the number fluctuates as mine did, please know that stupid little square is incapable of taking anything into consideration while you are standing on it. Our bodies change daily, even hourly, after you eat, after drinking water, during your period, if you haven't pooped today, before a workout, after a workout, or even if you moved your scale to another room. ALL these things affect that number.

Please allow me to take back my comment in the beginning of my book about how I wasn't going to give you any tasks to do. I'd like to change that by helping you get your freedom back and ask you to please get up right now and throw your scale into the garbage and let it be destroyed! Please don't be an asshole and give it to someone else, so they can be miserable! You are so welcome! Exhale a giant sigh of relief knowing that C-U-NextTuesday is out of your home and out of your life *forever!*

Balance

I've talked about listening to my body and trusting that my body knows what to do and how to do it. I can't stress that enough. I really had to think about how much of my day was spent thinking, talking, analyzing, shaming, stressing out about my body and how it looked to everyone else. It was all-consuming, and I was fed up with giving something so much energy. I really didn't want that for myself anymore. I realized that I've been searching for balance and everything that I was doing to myself every hour of every day was only driving me further away from finding it. I was making this too hard.

So I had to get still, stop torturing myself, and just breathe. Then, in the momentary stillness of my inner chatter. I was able to ask myself, what do I really want? I see clearly now that I have been influenced my entire life by dieting and workout advice from every possible angle. I know how difficult it can be to go against what you've been taught your whole life about how you should live it.

I realized my body gained and lost weight over and over because I didn't trust it. My body was protecting me from myself. I imprisoned my body for decades and continually forced it to be something that it wasn't. The real gift that I gave my body was unconditional love and the freedom to do what it was created to do—*live!*

My Body Can't and Won't Look Like Your Body

I can't count the number of times in my professional career as a personal trainer that I have felt *less than* because I don't have the body you see promoted as ideal on TV or in magazines. This has been such a long journey. It's taken a while to figure out my body and what it needs and to be comfortable with how it's going to look. The fantastic thing is I accept this a little more easily every day, but more importantly, I do believe that my body doesn't have to look like yours or like the women in the magazines.

I know I've been told how important it is for my body to look like a personal trainer. I've been body shamed in my industry many times. But I will re-emerge into this field post COVID with confidence, not only in my body, but in my capability to help others along the road to recovery. I know that I am naturally a good teacher and an empathetic woman, but what will make me an even better personal trainer is that I can relate to you, knowing that I've been in your shoes my entire life. Having an ally in this process can be priceless.

I am so happy that I'm starting to see some evolution in normalizing all bodies. Real women and men are choosing to put themselves out there. *Finally,* I can name a few clothing companies such as NIKE, Athleta, and Good American that are showing real women in their ads and actually making clothes that fit and look great! I'm so happy to see this happening in my lifetime. I have faith that normalizing ALL body shapes and sizes is here to stay, and I'm so proud to be a part of it.

IT'S MY JOB TO TALK ABOUT MY BODY

In this book, I talk about my body, and I will continue to do this in the future in both personal trainer mode and nonprofessionally. Navigating the difference between talking about my body in a degrading way and talking about my body as a matter of fact is new for me, and a little uncharted. How I do that in the future is so important to my long-term recovery from having a negative body image. I must be able to see myself as whole person, not just a body. I once had a whole dialogue of horrible things to say about my body on repeat. I truly see now how that only reinforced how I saw myself and how this dialogue continued the cycle for so long.

However, I also know that never talking about my body ever again isn't realistic. The things I say about my body now are much kinder, but in those tough moments, I need a gentle reminder to give myself a break when the negative wants to slip out to say, "I'm fat," or some other nasty thing. This will take time.

I'm learning that I can now talk about specific body parts and musculature because I'm cueing an exercise and use my own body as a positive example. Before when I would do that with a client, I would always start my sentence with a smart-ass remark like "if I had a bicep muscle" or "squeeze your glutes when you squat; don't let it jiggle like mine."

In my experience, women are incapable of speaking kindly about their bodies; we always have to say something negative about them. I hope to successfully spread the message that it's okay to talk about your body in a positive way. It's inevitable that we bring up our bodies in conversation, but we can do it with kindness. Let's all learn how to take a compliment for fuck's sake! I can discuss my past body image beliefs in a positive way now because it's my story and I lived it, but I also grew from it. It is gratifying to know it can help someone in the future.

Talking About Other People's Bodies

I'm seeing that normalizing real bodies has become the current trend on social media; many women and some men are out there saying *enough is enough!* I love being a part of this magical time, but I really hope that it gains momentum and becomes more than a trend. I hope it becomes a reality.

We need to allow ALL people to feel like their bodies are normal and healthy right now.

It's so fucking cool to finally see an abundance of people of every size and shape on every platform in our society. The conversation needs to stay open and positive, but real change is happening. There are so many amazing people doing their best every day to normalize real bodies. We have made a lot of strides, but we're not quite there yet. Let's stick together and continue to collectively move forward in that direction; our humanity deserves it.

It's also important to address the reality that some people still don't believe in the *healthy at every size* viewpoint, and they may still think it is okay to have opinions about your body. It will definitely happen to you and to me, but I hope everything I've shared with you in this book has shown you that you aren't alone. With self-love and acceptance, you can arm yourself with an invisible shield made of strength, kindness, and love.

When you present yourself to the world, there are things you can say and do when someone makes a comment on your body. I can only ask those of you who are reading this book to please be kind and respect other people no matter where they are on their journey. We don't need to judge people or be cruel. There are still people who aren't ready to stop restricting foods and dieting; they still believe that they must force their bodies into taking up the least amount of space possible. There are those people who may never understand that people in bigger bodies are healthy and happy and don't need to change for anyone or anything.

This is the hardest part of dealing with body image; our differences are more likely to drive a wedge instead of making us more compassionate. I want everyone to be free, but I also know how long it took me to get here.

Something I either heard or read has really stuck with me this past decade. It is this question: *Do you want to be right, or do you want to be happy?*

I offer that question to you when it seems difficult to accept someone else's truth. My promise to this movement is to continue to learn and grow, to be kinder and more accepting of all bodies. I hope you will too.

Giving Myself a Break

Today I can say I love my body and really mean it, but without having done the work, I know it wouldn't have been possible. I know I've mentioned this it in every chapter, but only because it's the hard truth. This process is going to take me as long as it takes. I still have my days when loving my body is hard. Knowing that I still have a lot of work to do, yet also how far I've come, helps me to stay in the present. The real difference for me is that I trust myself to keep going. I genuinely strive to love my body at whatever size it's going to land.

I can say *I love you* to my body with conviction, and my body shows me that it loves me back by feeling good and moving on its own without pain. I can tell by the way my body responds to the foods that I eat, and by the way my body moves through the everyday activities that I ask it to do, that I'm doing the very best I can. Even though I'm in a bigger body, it looks different than it ever has, which I know comes from my three pillars of nourishing, moving, and resting my body in the way that works for me.

Be patient and kind to yourself. Don't give up; don't expect your recovery to happen in an instant. You are going to have to commit yourself to staying open. I know you will have to address all those negative thoughts you have had about your body your whole life because that is what I had to do. I had to get very honest and raw with myself and declare: *I don't want to live like this anymore, and I want to be happy.*

I had to peel back the layers of who I thought I was supposed to be so I could uncover Who I Really Was. This definitely takes work and does not come easily. So please appreciate the process. Accept the process. And just go with the flow because every day is going to be different. Some days are going to be super easy. Some days are going to be super fucking hard.

I know there will be times when you think that it's easier to slip back into old behavior that is familiar and that makes you feel like you are in control. But I invite you to continue to push forward. I shared a few of my affirmations. Please feel free to use them.

I tell myself:

My body is beautiful.

I love you.

You're okay.

These words reinforce the idea that my body is perfect just the way it is right now. I'm constantly reminding myself that tomorrow is a new day and remembering how far I've come! Tell yourself whatever you need to get over that emotional barricade and keep going. It doesn't matter how corny you think soothing affirmations can be; it's so much better than hating your body and yourself.

My Story Is Your Story

I have shared the story of my many weight losses and weight gains and how I felt about myself during these times; I am sure that you can relate to me. I know what it's like to not feel safe in my own body, and what it's like to feel so uncomfortable at a bigger size and, surprisingly enough, in a smaller body too.

I couldn't love my body regardless of the array of sizes I had been over the years, and I thought for sure no one else understood my struggle. I see so clearly that it was a constant drain of my life force for way too long, and I'm so thankful I don't believe that anymore. I also know that I had to experience all these lessons so I could be here, right now, sharing my experience with you.

My goal for this book is to make sure that whoever reads my story can finally realize that they are not alone. So many of us are constantly in our heads about our bodies; we feel like we are the only ones who deal with this shit on a daily basis. We assume everyone else must love their perfect bodies, and no one else could possibly understand the difficulty of getting or keeping that weight off!

My dream is simple but seems unattainable at times. We all come in different shapes and different sizes; not one of them means healthy or unhealthy. I am not a therapist or a doctor, and I don't claim to understand or know each person's struggle with their body. I can only share my story and tell you how my experiences shaped me.

I may never be able to pinpoint all the reasons for my struggle. I'm sure growing up without any women who had a positive body image plays a part, as did the constant exposure to thin women in movies, on TV, or in magazines. Becoming a personal trainer, as we've discussed, was an important part of my journey. Honestly, it doesn't matter how it happened; it just matters that now, I see myself in a new light. The way my body looked had been a negative thought every single day of my life, but now I choose to see my body through a place of positivity and love.

Dreams Do Come True

I have always wanted to write a book about my experiences regarding my weight *losses*, but I didn't realize how much more valuable it was going to be to talk about my weight *gains* and the ups and downs that my poor body has been through over these four decades. I'm so grateful that I was aware enough during this process to realize that my story wouldn't be complete without talking about all of it. It finally felt like the right time to tell my story when I could see that all my experiences throughout life were really a series of beautiful lessons—lessons that have been teaching me how to love my body inside and out.

I don't have to live in shame or feel like there is something wrong with me. I have learned to ask for forgiveness from those I've hurt and to forgive those who hurt me. I learned to forgive others for what was said about me and my body, and I forgave myself for believing that I haven't always been in the right body. I really hope that my book is a message of true love and acceptance.

Let's continue to discuss the topic of both body weight and body image until the negativity attached to it is a thing of the past. I keep thinking how amazeballs it's going to be that future generations of girls and boys won't even know what it's like to think of themselves as fat. This awful stigma of body size has been keeping us unhappy and making us feel unlovable for way too long. It has to *stop!*

I've learned that my recovery had to start with me. I had to break my own cycle and live life for myself. I want to pay it forward now and help others see their own light. You, too, can have freedom from the fear of being fat or from being stuck on this diet roller coaster. Decide right now that you are in the right body and see how bright your own light shines. It's magnificent.

I met Rachel ten years ago when she walked into the gym I managed in Manhattan. My first impression of her was that she was kind, and when I saw her training her clients, I also saw how empathetic she was with them. Her empathy is like a salve to a wound, and her book will do the same for countless others.

— Steve

Conclusion

Thank you for reading my story. I know I told you countless times throughout this book how important it was to point out that you are not alone. You were never alone. We have spent either most or all of our lives hating our bodies, because we believed they weren't doing the one thing that they were supposed to do, be fucking small! The real beauty of all that frustration and pain is that there is finally a way out of that dark abyss. We can love and trust our bodies unconditionally!

Trust that food is here to nourish our bodies, not to hurt us. It absolutely should be a feeling of pure delight when we sit down to eat a meal, knowing that the intended outcome is to be satiated and full. Let's strive never again to feel disheartened at the sight of our reflections and never to refuse our picture being taken. Think about all the memories that we've missed out on over the years because of that, and let's not allow ourselves to miss another moment. We no longer should believe we aren't perfect the way we are right this second!

I've shared with you a few times that this it is not an overnight process; it takes time, possibly years, to unlearn all the beliefs and behaviors that you live by now. It took me decades of my life to be able to love myself and love my body and all its different parts. I know that I still have so many more lessons to learn. Those may never stop. Trust me; this is a process.

Reach out to me and other like-minded women. We are here to guide you, so please do not give up.

I have tried every diet and every exercise plan created by people. I have also reached out to many different people for their help. The most valuable thing that I learned through this journey—the advice that has worked better than any outside influence, and still works—is this: *You have to trust yourself.*

It is so wonderful to have a ton of resources to turn to for inspiration, books that you can read, and other people to share your experiences with. That's how we learn and grow. However, if your gut tells you some resource is not right for you, then it isn't. If any outside influence seems to be confusing you or making you feel unsure of yourself, I invite you to turn away and go down a different path. Allow yourself to trust your intuition, believe in yourself enough to say, "No thank you, I can do this myself."

When you've finished this book, set it down, exhale deeply, and go on your way with your head held high. If you go get a doughnut, or whatever your happy food is, whether you're walking down the street or the aisle of the grocery store, keep your head held high, knowing that you are beautiful, capable, and *whole!*

Next Steps

I have so many dreams for what can possibly come out of this book. I can't wait to start my weekly *Doughnut Diaries* podcast with many amazing guests who also share in this journey. I will always be available for interviews and speaking engagements to discuss my experiences about learning to see my body differently, and to help keep the conversation about body positivity going. I offer an online support program so you can break the chains of dieting with my help. Online or in-person cooking classes and one-on-one sessions are also possible.

Reach out to me at:

- RachelLavinFitness.com

- On Facebook, search for Rachel Lavin Fitness (facebook.com/rachel.lavin)

- Instagram @rachellavinfitness

About the Author

Rachel Lavin is a Certified Personal Trainer and a Certified Health Coach. She grew up in Northern California and has lived in Hawaii; Vancouver, Washington; and Portland, Oregon. She currently lives in New York City with her boyfriend.

Rachel has been teaching group fitness classes since 2000. She taught dance classes, aqua aerobics, stretch classes, Jazzercise, and corporate bootcamps until 2010. In 2006, Rachel graduated from Portland Community College with an associate's degree in applied sciences and became an ACE-Certified Personal Trainer. Currently, Rachel has been specializing in one-on-one personal training. Rachel creates a special bond with all her clients. It is important for her to be their teammate, as well as their cheerleader, while teaching proper exercise techniques.

Rachel has been recovering from restrictive diets and binge eating, and she really wants to share her story with the hope that she can reach as many people who have had similar experiences as possible. She wants to be an ally for the people all over the world with the hope that we can win this fight on how we see our bodies and learn to love our bodies unconditionally. Rachel believes that we are all in this together and no one is alone.

Made in United States
North Haven, CT
17 May 2023